I Find You in the *Stars*

MLIVV

Jessica Livia

1

ISBN: 978-1-962072-03-8

Cover art & design by: Melissa M. Combs

Octave
Eight
PUBLISHING
∞

octaveeightpublishing@gmail.com

I Find You in the *Stars*

MLIVV

Jessica Livia

Whatever our souls are made of,

his and mine are the same.

- Catherine, Wuthering Heights

Dedication:

Matthew Joseph Misiuk.

My husband, I'll always keep your memory alive.

I will find you every lifetime. I hope through my words,
our love story lives on forever. Thank you for this
beautiful life you have left me with, and the miracle
we created. I miss you every second of every day.

Til' we meet again.

I find you in the *stars*,
amongst infinite fireflies
that twinkle at dusk.

I find you in the *stars* amongst
the stories of love and of war
that create constellations we
map out in our minds as beauty.,

I find you in the *stars* amongst
the tales of forbidden lovers, punished,
sent to live in the endless vault of darkness.

I find you like a nightingale finds it's
voice to sing unchained melodies
to the *stars*, in hopes to find love…
just as I will one day find you amongst
the *stars*, in a constellation of our very own —
a constellation we will call *h o m e*.
Somewhere we will never be torn apart again.

I scream in silence,
reaching to be held by the ghost of *y o u* ;
searching a callus void in my soul.

I close my eyes, reach my hand out, and pray
to whoever is listening —

let
   me
      feel
         yo u
            once
               more.

I'll trade this salvation
to feel whole with *you* again.

It's the moon that reminds me of you.

Not for it's bright glowing beauty, but
the
jagged surface in which maps out
where
it's been hit; ***bruised.***

It reminds me of you for it's intricate
scars,
and how they connect together in a beautiful pattern that
the world marvels at.

You remind me of the moon because you too are as
alluring as the imperfect surface that poets and
authors have written countless tales about.

You too are an infinite muse.

You remind me of the moon because you radiate a beauty
my soul yearns for, yet you're too far to caress.

You remind me of the moon because you had a dark side
too; hidden from humanity,
yet people always stared in awe at your luminosity.

You remind me of the moon because no matter what
lifetime, I'll always find you, amongst the *stars*, and love
you just as all civilization will eternally be undyingly in
love with the moon.

Torn,
        bloody,
and ripped into tiny fragments,
I try to scrape what's left of my soul.

            Grievous,
I try to heap the pieces that make me whole.

I want to feel happiness,
but I don't know where to start.
It's a beginning with no end;
a constant struggle; a war of confusion
no one can mend.

For a moment I may smile,
but it doesn't mean the pain has subsided.
Scared of being chided for a smile I force
repeatedly, I try to think of happiness
and it always comes back to you.

If anyone ever tells you a person can't be your
happy place, I would argue, that's not true.

So how do I continue in a lemniscate of dismay?
I wish I could feel happiness again,
but this pain is here to stay.

Our love was **unrivaled**;
incomparable to any I've heard,
because it was ours.

And these words
I write,
I will scream into
the night sky
to be echoed
into Space's
consciousness,
so she herself can
weep in joy at such
beauty —

so the **magic**
we created
can be told light
years away.

There are dark forces pulling at my body,
relentlessly gathering in my subconscious,
rendering me to be ***immobilized;***
opening pandora's box in my mind,
releasing all evil.

My emotions are now disoriented.

They took the pen of my life and
bound my book tight with suffering.

"I love you."

"You promise?"

"I Promise."

Saying ***"I love you"*** was like
drenching my heart with gasoline.
Now I fear with one tear,
you will extinguish me entirely.

It's inevitable.
There is no *after you.*
I don't even remember my life before you.
You hit me like a whirlwind, then engulfed me in a
typhoon of devotion with my love,
permeating through my veins.

I'll travel into oblivion for eternity *with you.*

When you fall asleep tonight,
remember we lay under the same *stars*,
and carry the same scars.

Living perpetually in love;
inevitably, my **Twin Flame.**

My mirror soul, together we are ascending to a
higher frequency, because now that we found each other,
we
     are
        whole.

You asked me how much
I love you.
I should respond with a **wildfire of words,**
but I'm quiet.

Because, how do I explain to you a
love so deep it consumes me down to my
very cells; or how **it** (your love) is a ribbon
around my DNA?

It's my whole being.

Her passion was misunderstood for weaknesss.
But she was anything but feeble.
She faced struggle and was constructed of scars beautifully
aligned, like the constellations radiating the night's sky.

She was a ***bewitching***
confliction of a tortured soul.

If you were a verse in a song,
I'd keep you on *repeat* just to feel
each vibration of your voice play
over again inside of my mind.

Your words make me *complete*.
They take me back to a time where innocence
was pure and love was so much more.

Losing you was like the
Titanic being ripped in two
and separated at the bottom
of the ocean.

You were my
greatest voyage;
the journey
I will forever be lost on.

You were my vacation from reality;
the flight I'd stay on **forever** with no destination,
but straight *into your arms.*

You were my feeling of wanderlust,
because next to you,
I was able to be **everywhere,** *all at once.*

I'm forgiving trust.
It's not it's fault others broke it.

I'm putting back the pieces and
filling in it's cracks; giving it
as my masterpiece to someone who
will see it for it's full beauty and appreciate
it's cracked edges.
Someone worthy.

I give you my trust, put back together by
my very hands.
Please don't break it.

I need you right now, *I do.*
I'm lost *without you.*

The ghost of your presence is haunting me.
It's like a scary movie I can't shut off.
I'm engulfed in your memory, your scent,
and your touch.

It's all hitting me in waves
and I feel as if I'm drowning.
But the reality is worse —
that no matter how hard I try and fight this feeling,
I cannot, because you imprinted on me.

I'll feel you *always,* so how can I handle the pain?
I feel it with every part of my being.

I've heard once, it takes courage to let go,
when in reality, I'm letting go of so much more —
a part of me.

But the gallantry here is learning how to live
incomplete.

The only thing between us is the veil.
I feel it *thinning.*
I feel *you beside me.*
I feel it becoming *frail.*

I put my hands on it,
and feel yours touching mine.
For a moment, you're next to me.
 Like the moon raising the tide —
I feel your pull from the other side.

I would rip out my own heart if it meant
keeping yours from feeling pain.
To protect your mind, I'd quite literally go insane.
There's nothing I wouldn't do to ensure
your survival.

Maybe it makes me crazy, but if you needed my
breath, *I'd breathe my final.*

Your sanguine touch mesmerized me.
It felt like holding hope.
And the confidence
that radiated off of you indulged me.
You were buoyant, I was broken.
You were my antidote for the despondent
inferno in my mind.

You were
    infectious
        in a ***uniquely beautiful*** way.

My heart is now the remnants of a bomb
so gently assembled, but so catastrophically
b   l   o   w   n
into nothing but tiny pieces,
with only nanoscopic parts left
to even know it ever existed at all.

We may not have
traveled the world,
        sailed the seven seas,
 or climbed the tallest mountains,
but we've *always* had one another.

And that *love* transported
us to some of the most
beautiful dimensions,
with worlds others may never see.

My words flow through you,
tether themselves around your feral heart,
then bleed through me.

You are my every creation;
my sanity;
my salvation.

I sat there singing a song to the moon.
That's when the universe realized he was singing
the same rhyme too.

He was a world away,
but under that same full moon.

Lovers meant to love from afar.
The night was their solitude.

They signed their name in the *stars,*
eternally dedicated to one another.

No matter the distance.
No matter how far.

You are my greatest rapture
and legion of pain.
An anomaly of love.
A beautiful configuration of a tormented soul,
conflicted by wounds, stitched together with good
intentions; sculpted with a beautiful smile.

I'm
   f
      a
         l
            l
               i
                  n
                     g,

knowing I will bruise,
but willing to take the pain if you're there
while I heal.

You're an ***obsessive liar***,
            and I'm a ***wildfire.***
We were doomed from the start.
You fueled me with passion, though it was short lasting.

I PROMISED I'D TAKE YOUR BREATH AWAY.

Each word written like
dripping *stars*, burning
hydrogen into helium.
My skin glowing,
creating sonnets.

My love for you is creating
galaxies.

Your love awakened me as if it was
the first ray of light on a raven horizon —
sand in my eyes and between my toes.
You're the only one who knows the depth
to my shallow waters, because you didn't tiptoe
but you dove right in, absorbing all of my sin.
Hands locked while the sun rises,
together we lay as the sky turns from black to blue;
the world awakening as my soul does from
touching you.

This is spiritual and so much more than lust.
Just don't let go.

I'm bad at goodbyes.
I think of letting go and then I see the swirling colors of
brown and green in your eyes —
a kaleidoscope so intoxicating
it's as beneficial as the air I breathe.

I picture it,
        eyes closed,
                heart pounding,
                        my eyes drowning.

I can't let go.

You're still what excites me.
And I hope they all see the way the moon pulls
the tide, and the sun shares its rays.

I'll continue loving you til my last day.

I'll never say goodbye…
but with a sigh, I will whisper
"I'll see you soon."
Like the warmth of June,
you surround me.
I'm still engulfed in your being;
passion still screaming
for a touch I'll never feel.
But as I kneel
head in my hands
on the bed,
the one thing I know
is our love story,
though it was quick
like two wicks burning one flame,
it will be
one of the greatest stories of all time,
as I tell it, one rhyme at a time.

I want to thank **Time** for all that it has given me.
You see, too many people are quick to say time is a thief,
yet the only thing stolen is appreciation for the moment.
We are quick to blame time when tragedy strikes, saying
there wasn't enough, yet not show gratitude towards the
moments that
made the love that created such grief.
You have to have had the time to love in order to have
loved and lost.
Time is not a thief.
Time will always continue on like the spirit within you. Be
kind and grateful to both; they are everlasting. Don't blame
time. **Blame greed.** Don't let greed mislead. Time is a
luxury in this world; it's perception, through self
discovery.

"But what happens when you see him with someone else?"

I'll always love him, and when that love is pure and true you put that person above your own feelings.
Sure, it will be bittersweet.
Part of me will wish I was her, but the better part of me will smile just because he's smiling.
Even if I'm not the one who put my favorite smirk there and it was for... *her.*

Like a siren she called out to the sea,
singing a song she wrote for me.
Hymns of unfathomable enchantments.
A *goddess of seduction.*
Coming to her was my destruction.

A modern day
𝕽𝖔𝖒𝖊𝖔 and 𝕵𝖚𝖑𝖎𝖊𝖙.
I prayed we didn't end up in regret.

But passion ignited,
and lit the path straight to destruction.
The story of tragedies,
            now both our realities.

I write letters to you *every night,*
burying them at *daylight,*
with hopes the heart sings my poems
and the wind carries my words
straight to you.

Grief is as grey as clouds bearing rain.
You carry it like a ball and chain.
There are moments of **black,** where you feel
nothing but intense agony,
then, moments of **white,** where for a
split second you see clarity.
It's a back and forth struggle of emotions.

So I can only say I know for sure,
if grief were a color, **it would be grey.**

One single tear
fell down my eye,
like one
beautiful snowflake
falling from the sky,
laying on a blanket of white,
cradled by the lull of night.
The frigid wind hums
melodies in my ear;
an orchestra of
snowfall singing to me.
I finally let go,
now ***I'm free.***

From broken dreams
and heartfelt cries,
I wanted nothing more
than to take your pain,
carry it with me like
a ball and chain.
Because I knew without you,
I'd never be the same.

In the end I never thought you'd become just another
story; a memoir of a time the moon shined brighter and the
birds flew in conjunction with the wind; a time there were
cotton candy clouds in the sky.

And when you said I was ***beautiful,***
    I didn't feel insecure as to ask why.

A time when you made me see the beauty in
a spider web, or how a drop of water makes a
perfect bubble, or how not all pretty faces like yours
are the cause of trouble.
I never thought you'd become my most beautiful
chapter —
where life was ***loved*** and I was ***full of laughter.***

He was stuck
in his own hell,
imprisoned by his mind.
Broken, he tried to love a girl,
and that's
how an **angel** *died.*

Shadows shrouding me;
this hex encompassing
a love I cling to.
Jealous eyes lay waste
to something so flawless.
Stringent, I fight spite,
but those jealous
eyes become more malicious.

You're taken away.
Alone, I lay in
unjust madness,
stranded eternally
at the Graceland of sadness.

As I wait for these waves to carry me away,
praying the waters purify my tainted mind,
I feel the riptide;
therapeutic like white noise,
pulling me into a tv screen.
And still I pray I'll see deliverance by dawn.

I didn't need to speak.
My tears echoed all around me.
My blank stare with tears pouring down
spoke the volume needed.

I wanted to go; ***I didn't know where.***

My body didn't feel real.
I wanted to hide.
I felt my spirit slowly dying.
You had a spot perfectly carved into my soul.
I had it ripped apart,
carrying my heart,
this is now where we woefully part.
I'm not sure how to survive ***without you.***

I never found it coincidental that destruction
and destiny both start the same.
Because I've come to find when it's your time,
destruction and destiny *collide...*
as if they were always the same to begin with.

She was so complex
she saw living and
the inevitability of dying
both equally beautiful;
triumph and *tragedy*.

This pain
is sharp,
penetrating my skin like a needle,
hitting the vein,
piercing it,
*sucking the **life** out of me.*

I lay here and I listen to the rain
drenching the soil,
continuing life,
the earth still spinning;
*the universe just **orbiting** my pain.*

Round and round like a carousel,
I ride in distress,
and I must confess
forfeited now,
I'm getting used to this
*harrow **horror** story.*

I became an innocent hostage to devotion.
There is this notion that loyalty is essential,
but let me express, not everyone will honor your sacrifice
of being faithful.
Some will actually use it against you.

Don't become the person you used to know
over a love fabricated from lies and denial.

The same way a knife cuts your skin quickly and easily,
you can't let fidelity let a narcissist win.

Don't be scared.
It's okay.
I'll see you one day, like fireworks
shooting in the night sky.
We will meet like fire meets the fuse;
our souls will merge, and in an instant
we will spark eternity with our love entombed.

The sky will boom,
*while **our story** echoes*
through all of time.

I thought I could stop fate.
What a tragic lesson I learned,
soaking in tears I've cried;
years of yearning for you,
lonely and *scared.*

I can create oceans with my eyes,
yet what I long for is in the *stars,*
amongst the somber space above.

My grief, heavy like waves crashing down on me.
But I will build a rocket out of passion,
everlasting with your picture in my pocket,
I'll forgive fate.
But please wait for me... *I'll find you again.*

We got the lyrics wrong.
We should have been the most ***beautiful song***.
We both longed for a love out of this world;
a love where we belonged in rows of thorns and thistles,
full of our
lyrics,
       roses, and
             pistols.

I'll pick you the best flower.
Your bottom lip, soft and sour,
with a kiss, so deadly.

I wasn't ready to finish the song so soon, but with you
humming our tune, I'll accept our final kiss.

Oh this love, ***I'll miss.***

It's time to take our final bow.
Our song, though it was wrong,
it had the most beautiful sound.

You fall in love with
a *poet's* words before
their appearance.
You feel their emotions,
their pain, and happiness.
Holding their words is
like holding them tight —
the way you embrace
each word like a hug.
You have a chance to peak
into their soul and study their mind;
to fall in love with someone
who wears their *heart on their sleeve,*
and spills their entire being onto paper,
naked and bare for you to see.
Such beautiful vulnerability.

One of the most courageous things
I'll ever do is finally let go of you.
It'll hurt my soul, but I am holding on to
old memories and not making new ones.
I'm stuck in the past, forever wishing
we would last.
*But times going **fast**.*

So I promise I'll carry a part of you in
everything that I do.

Everything about you ,
I've never come across in anyone before.

The way you radiated a sort of loving energy
uplifted spirits by having the super power to
make everyone laugh.

You saw *light* where others saw *darkness.*

Your spirit was contagious,
and I swear there are moments I can feel you.
I don't know if it's really you,
or the imprint you left here, but either way,
I'm grateful when I feel it.

I will hold you and dance with you again.
Until then, ***I'll just pretend.***
I'll close my eyes and picture your
hand locked in mine,
my head against your chest,
and feeling your heartbeat pounding,
saying:
"I love you"
and me saying, like always,
"I love you most."

I promise I'll never stop dancing,
even with your ghost.

I was crestfallen,
bound by limitations
and the mysteries of the unknown;
wary of consequences
trapped in my body.
My spirit restless,
endless, searching for **him.**
A dream traveler,
searching countless constellations.
Guided by each *star* gleam,

love fueled me.
Passion guided me.
Distance, insignificant.
Bound to **him**; souls interlaced.
Even if it takes me til the end of time,
hearts aligned, **I'll hold you again.**

I don't want to do today.
Not in the physical sense, but mental.
My mind is wrapped in daydreams that
never can be, and in holidays, and heartfelt
smiles I'll never again see.
Reminders of the time you've been gone,
my soul, tired and desolate.
I'm reliving moments;
memories that we did share.

I find solace in our memories because after all this time,
you still grab me by the soul.

I got sucked into your energy field
like a whirlwind.
Our energy fused
into one,
and something
magical happened,
down to a cellular level.
Together our vibrations
started healing the trauma
of past afflictions.
Together, *we healed.*

God made you for me,
and what a ***beautiful*** job he did.
He put every one of my favorite things
together, and I found it all in you.

Your hair,
your eyes,
your mind.

Theres no surprise,
*how your **crazy** matched perfectly with mine.*

The day you died
I don't remember much.
It's true in traumatic situations you black out.
I remember the sun wasn't shining,
and I remember the sound of sirens.

I didn't get to you in time,
the police got there first.
I tried to break past them, screaming crying
*(that memory is truly the **worst**.)*
They held me back trying to stop my screaming.
I remember just thinking
if I could get to you
I could put the air back into your lungs,
not realizing how wrong I was.

You were taken away.
I never got to say goodbye.
They didn't come get me
to kiss you one last time.
I hope you now know how hard
I fought to get to you.
I told you, if you leave me,
you will truly destroy me.

I will never be okay in this life again.
Every word I said was true,
because ever since that day,
no matter how much I pray,
no matter what anyone says,
*I will **never** be the same.*

I got to love you like a shooting star,
immensely, exquisitely, and hastily.
You were the most beautiful thing I had ever seen,
yet gone in the blink of an eye.
But that moment of time; the flash of an instant
will be etched into my being ***eternally.***

I belonged to you
multiple lifetimes before.
I know this to be true
because the day we met,
my soul already knew.

It smiled and said,
"I told you I'd find you."

Come to me in my dreams,
haunt me if you must.
Just don't leave me in this treacherous
landscape to walk alone.

Don't leave me in my madness,
to bathe in tears of sorrow,
to wrinkle alone.

*Come to me in **any form.***
Surround me in a storm of energy,
*just **don't** leave me.*

If you should go before I,
wait for me at the bleak of time.

Any lifetime,
any fate,
we'll walk into together.

Destiny will narrate
whether we walk into the sun
or merely step
into obvlivion.

Wait for me.

I'll find you hand in hand,
side by side.
*We'll walk into **eternity** together.*

I'll wait for you,
pen in hand.
I'll finish our story.

*It began with **you**,*
*it'll end with **me**.*

I'll keep you alive forever
through words;
what a purpose you served.

You saved my life.
Now I'll write yours into infinity,
and sign it:

- *the girl who got to love you.*

"Please stay."
I remember I repeated those words
in my head at least a thousand times.
There was no way to prepare myself for goodbye.
I wanted you forever, but forever came fast,
and forever didn't last.
But still, in denial, I utter *"please stay,"*
in hopes one day you'll come and say,
"I'm sorry love, for the delay."

In case you don't know
I'm crazy about *you,*
thunderstorms,
and everything ***halloween.***

But you're the aesthetic
I can live in *forever.*
My favorite colors and hues
all shine out of *you.*

You loved me til the end of your life.
Now my love,
I'll love you til the end of mine.
I ask for a sign, but isn't the greatest sign
of all the love we will eternally share?
Let that love wrap its arms around
you *til' I can* **again.**

The moment we locked eyes
it's no surprise it was a
stellar collision here on earth.
I swear the ground shook.
One look,
and I radiated a light that leaked out of every
broken crack,
and then I knew my life purpose was back.
*I just stared into the eyes of **my destiny.***

I must have slipped into a reality where you never left.
Because you walked through the door, slipped your hand
in mine, and with that smirk said "come on babe."
I wasn't going to question *how or why.*
I didn't care. I just stared at you, tears falling from my
eyes. In silence, I jumped into your arms, you caught me
once more, and the only words I got to utter were *"I'll
never let go this time."*

You'll always be my *forever.*
I waited a lifetime for you,
now I have to wait another.
But no matter how long,
no matter what lifetime,
it'll *always be you.*
I'll find you again.

The divinity of our last kiss made even the most famous poets struggle to find a way to explain something so *heavenly.*

All these tears I've cried,
it's my heart that died.
So let me freeze time
before it's too late.
With love in my heart,
you are ***never-ending***.
I thought your death would kill me,
but I'm still here.
I did not become stronger.
Life now only seems unwillingly longer.
I hold on to what remains of you;
I cling to the mere fact you existed —
that such a handsome boy
with his whole life before his eyes
was once here.
Death, you can deny it,
but that only creates anger.
Why was I given something so beautiful
to just be taken away?
*You deserved **longer**.*
*You deserved **better**.*
*We should be **together**.*
Right now, wherever you'd want to be.
I would have taken you anywhere
just to see you smile.
There's so much you never got to see.
You never made it on an airplane…
now every time one passes,
I see your dreams fly by,
*along with **mine**.*

How do I put you on paper;
something so numbingly beautiful.
*How do I express **you?***

You spoke of scars *as if* we didn't obtain them together. Mapped out like an old world map of places that no longer exist, of battles long ceased.

You spoke *as if* I didn't know each intricate wound; *as if* I wasn't at the battle beside you; *as if* together we didn't carry the same patterns of dejected sorrows; *as if* I didn't try to take each bullet for you; *as if* I didn't try to carry each burden; *as if* our love alone didn't conquer the immortality of an unjust world.

Written in blood and signed in fervor,
you're my life preserver.
I sign myself to you eternally,
my being, body and soul.
You stole my beating heart
and seized my spirit.
It was God's will.
You can't fight fate,
but why try when what you have
is unquestionably utter *utopia?*

I sit here all alone in the dark fighting shadows, gripping my hair, elbows on my knees.
I keep repeating *"please."*
I didn't want it to end this way, but some things you can't go back to, cause you let them slip away.
Back pressed against the door;
the wood splintering my spine;
hands holding the water spilling from my eyes.
They were never lies.
I always loved you, but insecurity struck.
I feel stuck,
not in this relationship, but in my head.
I feel so confined.
*I promise it's not you, **it's in my mind.***

I dance around with my eyes closed,
playing your favorite song,
reliving each elated moment.
Each lyric spilling from my lips
with a melancholy twist,
while memories flood my eyes;
time flies.
*I'll **never** stop dancing with you.*

You held my hair in your fist and pulled
me to your lips so intensely and with all you had.
I remember you told me,
*"I'll never **love** another, like **I love you.**
Never."*
I hope that's still true.
I hope no angel up there has caught your eye.
I can't deny, I'm jealous of the divine all around you,
all because they're within your embrace.
I hope when my time stops,
we travel the constellations one *star* at a time.

Together I hope, I pray I'll always, in every lifetime be the
girl you'll never replace.
*In **this** life and **the next,***
So wait for me in that incandescent light aglow.

Her:
"My love, what if death comes and separates us?"

Him:
"Death may come and wrap its warmth around me decaying this skin I'm in, but my soul will still be watching every sunrise with you. My spirit will be the wind running through your hair, as my fingers once did. I will wait if need be, because we have loved endless lifetimes before, and will love endless lifetimes more. *I will always find you.*"

And in the end, the temporary cure will kill you.
But cut me open and
fill me with your poison.
If never feeling your touch is the punishment,
fill me with damnation.

Insidious he was in every way,
deceptive from day one,
heedless of anyone's feelings
but his own.
I knew he'd be my demise, but lust got in the way.
And all I can say is it was a
*bittersweet **fall from grace.***

I embraced my fears,
grabbed his face,
and kissed him.
He was going to be my demise
when our lips touched.
I heard the trumpet of doom
but holding him, it was inevitable —
our love was so strong together,
we'd make the **heavens fall.**

The night we fell in love, it turned cold.
I didn't realize I had sold my soul.
You were an angel in my eyes.
I didn't see your wings
stitched on —
what a tragically **beautiful** disguise.

At first I was scared to love you.
I was never one to love small.
It was all consuming, soul shifting love,
or nothing at all.
I put the fear aside, and I can't lie,
you shook me to my very core.
*But I got to **love you**.*
Rip roaring, tide shifting,
your embrace, uplifting.
*I got to **love you** against all odds.*
Together we aligned with the Gods,
setting forth the second coming.
Our love was so strong the universe shook,
but it didn't matter.
With one look, *I got to **love you**.*
Scared of being consumed in a love too grand,
fate wrote our story by hand,
and *I got to **love you**.*
I loved you too strong for this world,
so the angels came and made it brief.
Time is all we needed, but she was a thief.
But *I got to **love you**.*
That love still lingers today.
I hope these words convey the
magnitude of my love for you,
because miracles were created.
You had to leave;
it was fated; frustrated.
I'm just honored *I got to **love you**.*

I sometimes wish I cried tears of sulfur
so I'd dissolve this skin I feel trapped in.
Living without you feels like punishment.
*I'm a skeleton of who I **once was,***
over a love I cherish undyingly.

Each tear I cry is a memory of you.
Our story, it pours from my eyes.
These memories relived everyday,
one tear at a time,
I keep you alive
in the hardest way.

They say when it's dark enough,
you can see the *stars*.

For me, in the pitch black,
I can feel your hand run down my back.
I can hear your voice.
But since you left,
the only solace I feel is in the absence of light.

And I was the girl that got
to love you briefly,
but potently.
You were soul consuming;
intoxicating.

You were the high I'll
forever be in recovery from.

I wish I could open the door to a black abyss
where I can feel ***nothing***,
especially the excruciating thought of our last kiss.

Each agonizing moment, they tell me is grief.
All of every second truly is denial and disbelief.

His fingertips running up and down my back,
the weight of his burdens intertwined around
my legs.

I felt the heaviness he carried, yet he was so delicate with
the way he placed his hands on me.

*His beauty, **ethereal**.*

The way his chestnut hair fell towards his almond eyes, he
radiated such an alluring light, while carrying such a deep
darkness.

The perfect symmetry of his face could bring even the
most beautiful angels to their knees.

I need to bleed these words to heal.
I need to open the wound,
let the words pour out,
see the crimson stain the pages,
as my tears stain the floor.

Acceptance is the hardest part,
but the most crucial stage of grief.
But I promise
*you'll **live on** through my words.*

The day you demise,
take my flame
and use your last breath
to burn it out.
My soul was never meant to
endure without you.

The pain is agonizing.
The memories are all that's left.
You always promised to love me
in this life, and the next.
So wait for me in the luminous light.
We will be together again,
when the time is right.
Your soul will find mine.
*We are **forever** intertwined.*

We would lay in bed
while he traced the constellations
around my body,
telling me stories about *how I was the* **sky,**
and *he was the* **moon.**

How like the *stars.*
I kept shining,
even when he wasn't there.
How nothing can dim my light.

In fact, he loved how without his light
I shined **even brighter.**
So when he disappeared,
like a new moon,
he came back trying to tell me
it was just a phase.

I loved every blood vessel broken in your eyes;
from **broken dreams** and **heartfelt cries,**
I wanted nothing more than to take your pain —
carry it like the clouds carry the rain.

We were introverts.
We loved to be left alone,
but only alone together.
We found **solace** *in* **solitude.**
Maybe our souls were the same
because together,
isolated away from the world,
our unity calmed our spirits.
Being alone with each other,
we found our home
amongst the quiet twinkling *stars.*

We became
synchronous ***loner lovers.***

Her scarlet hair shining in the moonlight;
he never saw such raw, natural beauty,
like Mother Nature sculpted her.

An enchantress of the night,
he lit up a path sending her directly to him.

But she liked
the stain of the **darkness** *on her soul.*
She felt solace in the calamitous unlit Greenwood,
for the moonlight alone sang unfathomable rhymes
to her.

I never wanted to live without you,
or accept a fate so cruel.
I fought and fought,
*I was **such a fool.***
I loved you without limit,
with a love so strong time stopped
that minute.

Since then,
the world continued to spin,
but I remained still —
frozen in the moment
***before** you, and **after** you.*

My soul won't rest til' it finds you everyday.
*It's pulling out of me to search for **you**,*
leaving me an empty vessel,
but thats better than the pain I feel when it returns.

Without you, it's war I face everyday;
a constant battle of a soul just trying to find
it's way home.

I don't want to swim in your love,
or bathe in your essence, only skin deep.
I need to *drown deep in **your soul.***
I want to *get lost in **your abyss.***

"I'll never leave you."
Four words I swore to be true; *s o   t r u e .*

I gave my entire being to you —
my mind, body, and spirit, intertwined with yours.
*It was a deathless **damnation.***

It was a cold, cruel fate that awaited us.
We were far from saviors;
sinners merely surviving this callous world together.

Darkness separated us,
but I knocked on deaths door,
*kicking and screaming to **let me in.***

Strip me of my skin and allow me to travel the unknown
with you —
even somewhere so cold and dark is home,
while our hands are locked together.

Forever,
with one last kiss as you draw the last ounce of vivacity
from me, we will travel the crossroads towards the endless
white light.

Take out the shovel.
*My **hopes** all passed away.*
All that's left is a corpse radiating dismay.
I'll take the shovel and bury them deep within
the abyss of my soul.

Maybe in our next life,
you'll unearth them and keep them as your own.
Til then, I'll water them with my tears.

"Til death do us part."
We took that out of our vows.
We said always, no matter what,
"in this life and the next."
Death came, but *"always"* stayed.

No matter what.
Forever.

When the last of us are
left here roaming the ruinous abyss,
my light will find yours.
Our souls will collide.
We will morph into one,
boundless.
Our love will travel
the constellations.

I never got to say goodbye,
but I think I wasn't meant to.
Because goodbye would mean the end
of **our story** *that is still continuing.*

Now we are in two different places;
different realms, yet still somehow we coexist.

And I know when my time comes,
you'll be there with that smirk saying "hey"
like you never even left.

I know all this love we had, it was on a spiritual level.
So that love will spiral together and intertwine.
We will travel into the next life where there
*we will find each other **in love** again.*

There was something about you;
something **divine.**
Perhaps the way your soul met mine,
the curvature of your smile,
or the way you shuttered each line.

Like watching cotton candy clouds on
a warm summer day, I knew wholeheartedly
with you,
my soul would always be okay.

"Tell me your story"

Where do I start? It's a deep story.
Probably not a tale as old as time,
because prince charming didn't stay.
But it's a true story of love,
extreme passion, suffering, resilience,
trauma, utter devotion, then devastation.
*It's a story **I wear on my skin,**
and a story **you can see in my eyes.***
My story taught me to never think it can't get
any worse, because the universe will show you just how
wrong you can be.

But I'm still here.

I survived so far, and throughout it all;
the horrid and the happy,
I wouldn't change one chapter of the story.

Even the most beautiful things fall in fury.
So as I fall from grace, the only silver lining
is maybe I'll be as beautiful and magical as the
shooting *stars* you search for.

Maybe you won't have to search no more.
Maybe you'll stare at me and finally say,
*"Oh how **lovely** you are."*

I'd take on the sea,
the currents,
ice burgs,
and cold,
just to be told
it wasn't true that you died.
And your life, it wasn't through.
You knew I'd move
heaven and hell
for you;
part the seas and try to give my self up in
retribution.
Screaming on my knees,
you knew I couldn't be
anywhere you wouldn't be.
I breathed you.
Now you're gone with no air source,
but I don't know how I'll survive.
I guess time hasn't yet stopped for me,
so I'll try.
You said you found what you loved and you'd
live for it it, *for me.*
You lied.

And now, without you,
I don't know how I'll exist or how to be me.

The only thing left I can do is
take each last ounce of air
from each memory and breathe
you back into life;
breathe you into the air around me,
so once again you surround me.

I need to feel you.

I can't accept our last embrace,
or the future without your face.
So I take what's left of you.

Surround me in an eternal hug,
and please don't let me go.
Because this life without you,
I truly don't want to know.

I close my eyes.
I picture you here, sitting on your bed with your favorite
beer, smiling, laughing, and full of life;
singing your favorite songs.
Telling me soon, I'll be your wife.

We were just kids at heart,
and I knew I loved you from the very start.
We had our whole life, I thought.
But that's not the lesson I was taught.

I wanted those days to last forever,
full of love, laughter and devotion.

*You will forever be **my favorite** emotion.*

I wish we got one last dance here on earth.
Gripping your shirt, pulling you close,
getting to kiss your neck, while you traced your fingers
down my back, hand in hand.

But if it's possible,
*wait for me where **forever** begins,*
and our souls will dance again.

He ran his hands down my back,
feeling each scar of my past.
His touch was enough to heal the pain
I held for decades.
His hands on my bare skin took all the wrong away.
As his hands ran up and down,
they casted a shadow from the flickering light.
He was slaying my demons one stroke at a time.
He was mine,
and now I would never with another
battle alone again.

My heart can't carry the name of another.
I can't think of another's kiss, or anyones smile.
People shrug it off and say *"it'll take a while."*
But it's been years and your favorite cologne still brings
me to tears.

I know some can move on, but I'm not them.
You're my rose and I'm the stem.
So though our petals have withered,
tears delivered, no one can take your place.
*Not one second **will I erase**.*
*Not one set of lips **will I taste**.*

I will wait til' forever starts again,
welcoming our first embrace.
Til then, I'll wait under the *stars*
in our favorite place.

I promise when you're weary,
I'll carry you to the next tune,
hold you as we dance under the moon.

I promise to be your strength when you are weak,
try to be all that you seek.
I'll do my best to help you stand tall,
and If ever you fall, hands locked,
I'll make sure we fall together.
I'll love you today, tomorrow, *forever.*

Through the sinister
darkness,
skulking
with reveling prospects
of our future;
with the demons casting shadows in my mind,
you shine your light so bright you doused them all —
my firefly.
Your light guides me even in the most stygian of times.

You were a tragic decision
that exploded *beautifully.*
The scattered memories
and shattered
glass; all fragments of my past.
Bad decisions
and broken promises
are now art that lay around
like a mosaic imprinted in time,
art for everyone eyes.

She talks to the moon,
       so the *stars* know her secrets.

He was ***my requiem,***
designed especially
for me.
Made of
the most pure intentions —
my sanctuary for sanity.

I have this box of your things.
I open it from time to time
to smell you and remind me
of when you were whole —
when you were vibrant and full of life.
This box full of shirts and a few small things
is my now my only way to feel you.
I remember the comfort of your hoodie —
the way the fabric felt on my skin
when you hugged me.
Now it's what I value,
left of you, in this bin.
For the rest of my days
I'll cherish what I have.
And when life gets tough
I'll put on your shirt,
try to stay strong,
and remember,
even with pain,
*I'll wrap myself in **your memory.***

*He is **my muse**.*
With every look,
he tells me a thousand words
that I can use
There is so much to say when I look his way.
*He is **a hundred books** left untold.*

Our love was a sonnet even Shakespeare could have never expressed. A story so rare even the best poets were baffled as how to share.

It was our ***love*** that set the way for the greatest stories of all time.

It was our ***story,***
the most famous poets used for their rhymes.

"What do you think hell feels like?"

"Traveling into the oblivion of his subconscious to be a memory; a bygone of a time I thought I mattered."
*But drugs **mattered more.***

All the words that echo in my head is all the pain
I've left unsaid. The memories bring me to tears.
I've missed so many years stuck inside my head laying in
anguish.
Sometimes I wish I was truly dead.
At least I'd be with you, at peace forever entombed.
But that isn't me or the person I aspire to be.
It is grief and the pain that consumes me.
So until I finally break free, if I ever truly can,
this is my new ***reality*** —
Living every day engulfed in grief, still in disbelief,
praying you send me strength;
*going any length **to find you once more.***

Like static on the radio, chaotic to hear,
the words **"he's gone"** rolled off their tongue and into
my chest, piercing part of my heart, severing a piece of my
soul he will forever carry with him.

I beat myself black and blue
fighting for a chance to love you.
I fought your demons.
I beat myself down, all trying to turn your life around.
I loved you without cost.
I just never understood how much pain you were truly in.
But every time you injected her into your veins,
she'd win.
I am sorry I couldn't save you,
no matter how hard I tried.
I hope you know all the false pleasure she gave you.
I hope now you know *she lied,*
No matter what, I will always love you without judgement.
Forever and always, in endless ways.

The real love of your life was never *those pills,*
nor those *little bags* that you falsified as giving you
thrills.

The real love of your life was the girl standing next to you,
drowning in tears,
fighting for your sobriety for years.
The real love of your life was never the high that you
searched for.
It was me, there loving you.
I can't deny and say I don't understand addiction,
because though she was yours, *you were mine.*
But she was the affliction.
She falsified her love to make you feel safe —
killing you slowly.
I loved you through every step, completely, and wholly.
Those drugs, they lied. But I tried.
I loved you too much to ever give up on you,
No matter if it took me down too.
She stole you away and I don't even have the words to
express the emptiness that I carry inside.
Still I try.

I sometimes wonder morbidly about your last breath. Were you scared, or unaware?

And why wasn't I there?

I ask the universe why no one let me hold you as you went away, but I didn't receive an answer.

I wonder your last thought
and if it was me.

I wonder if I could have stopped you,
or maybe some
things are really meant to be.
I question timing and death,
and if it's divine or a choice.
Bur all I know for sure,
is I really miss the sound of your voice.

A million lanterns being sent into the night sky,
lighting it like infinite fireflies with glimmering hope.
We always said this was one of our dreams to do, together,
to send a wish up to the heavens, but that was then; this is
now.

I'm here alone without you, and telling you I hope you can
see all you've missed since you left, as I imprint my lips
on the lantern and sent it up to the heavens.
Keep sending those repeating elevens.
*Our love, **not even death** could sever.*

What broke me is not that you left,
it is that you couldn't bare to stay.
What broke me is that I couldn't fix your pain, and that I
couldn't find a way to make you feel more sane.
What broke me is that I couldn't break you out of the
prison in your mind.
What broke me is I couldn't find a cure in time.
What breaks me repeatedly with the first light of dawn,
inescapably, *I didn't save you.*

I hate long car rides without you.
Everything seems to blur except the empty seat next to
mine, once filled with so much life, now empty and quiet.
My surroundings, desolate.
Headlights fading and blurring like tiny twinkling *stars.*
light years away. I now hate the highway because I no
longer hear you singing, no longer see you dancing;
I no longer have you.
Now alone, every ride, long or short seems like eternity
while I picture you there and smile in tears, reliving the
years that filled that seat blasting your favorite songs.
It seems so long.

Hollow inside, no light can seep in,
yet the sun beats down trying to douse me in warmth.
My soul, frozen.
The sun now hurts my grieving eyes.
Beautiful days hurt the most.
It's a reminder of the life you should be
living, yet my tears fall fast, sliding into my mouth, while I
choke on them.
*I fear I'll never see the sun
the same again.*

I Find You in the Stars · ★ MLIVV | *Jessica Livia*

I guess we did stare at each other
 too long the first night we met.
We got stuck somewhere between *disaster* and
something that could be ***absolute perfection.***

141

I wanted to thank you.
I'll always find home in the thought of our last embrace.
Though our love was short, *it was real.*
So real it imprinted into the sky like a meteor
traveling the Milky Way.
Like this meteor,
our love will always come blazing back around.
Our love did not die when you did.
It transformed.
Like the way I did.
Now I feel your love in the warmth of the sun,
the beauty in a bee resting on a flower,
the sand between my fingers,
and the sound of the waves crashing.
There is part of you in everything,
so *I'm never truly alone.*
I just miss the warmth off the body
I once called home.

I was a hopeful heart death shattered apart.
But love consumed me; ***intoxicated me.***
Now I lay afraid to be without you.
I let our memories invade my mind and remember why
every second with you is worth this pain.
I am condemned to be damned in this flesh contraption;
to keep replaying every second I spent with you.

His eyes erased the pain I had roaring in my soul.
Maybe it was the way
the crimson and bronze variegated.
Sometimes they even made the pain vanish.
If not for forever, at least for a short time.
And during that time I became "me," the person
I had been searching for since the ebony curse leaked into
the best parts of me.

His eyes were like an antidote, but like all fairytales at
midnight, the magic dissipated, and the light in his eyes
vanished as fast as it came... leaving me with the raven
plague that settled in my soul;
*leaving me **without him**.*

I look into our daughters eyes and I see you there
*in a **sparkle**; in a **spec**.*
I see you there in the way the colors amalgamate.
I see you in the way the light glimmers.
It creates a glow; a halo in her eyes as if you're reminding
me a piece of heaven is within her;
as if you're reminding me you shine through her eyes.
Our spirits are forever intertwined,
and I know
I'll find you ...
in her eyes.

I wanted a *forever* with you, yet here I am
living *forever without you.*
It's so cruel that something so absolutely
astonishingly perfect can be ripped away
in a mere instant.
What a cruel fate to have to live a life without you.

I'm sorry I couldn't save you.
God knows I tried,
but you slipped through
my fingers like sand in an hour glass.
Too fast to stop,
but I tried my hardest.
That last piece of sand fell
and I ran out of time.
It should be a divine crime to break apart a
love like ours.

My love,
I'm sorry I couldn't save you.

There is a road to my soul only you can travel to.
A ghost carriage carrying each tear I've cried in antiquated
luggage.
You carry my sorrow even in death,
as you travel the road back home to my soul;
back where you **belong.**

I wonder if she hears your screams
in her sleep, while she sits on her
mountain of remorse...
hearing your calls for help that she ignored.

I wonder if she thinks of the times she put poison
in your hands, with no regret,
while evil stared her in the face.

I wonder if she knows she handed you
her **demons;**
her past **traumas;**
her **self hate...**
all for you to carry on your own.
All to bring you down with her,
like a landslide.

She destroys everything in her path —
even your spirit that clung to her
in hopes for the comfort any child
searches for.
But it was never about love;
only ever about control.

I'll put my anger in a box and mark it hazardous.
Unleashing it will not be merciful.
I'll keep it away, but one tear.
Sometimes I fear the
vengeance for your death won't be just.
I'll keep it locked away, but yet again,
one day, everyone will pay for their sins.
Til' that day, I'll smile and say I'm okay,
because I know virtue will triumph
the jubilation my soul will one day render.

If I could have absorbed your pain,
I'd injection it into a tattoo.
I'd wear each moment of agony and despair.
I'd take it all from you and shoot it
into a vivid masterpiece.
I would have worn your agony **eternally.**

The moment they tell you
"we did all we can do"
your heart, mind, and soul are
eternally split into two.
Your life in a split second, divided into
before and *after* their death.

You drop to your knees
begging god to take your life instead,
and restore their last breath.
You *beg, bargain,* and *plead.*
Your heart bleeds the pain unbearable
and it's only them that you need.

With the complete accuracy that a
lightening bolt hits a tree,
you found me.

I find solace in the graveyard amongst the dead
that I once loved.
The withering tombstones decaying remind me of my
bones becoming fragile with each passing day.
The quietness.
I hear the call of restless spirits dying to be heard.
There is something metaphorically twisted about that yet
still here amid the quiet chaos, *I feel home.*
The longing I have to feel you once more.
Now six feet away doesn't seem so far.

Spiders spin shadows in my mind.
Webs of denial fall from sable colored walls.
Memories dance through these halls —
echoes of past smiles.
Cracks of contradiction crawl down the walls.

I became a haunted vessel since our last embrace.
This home inside me, no longer safe.
I created this prison —
embodied it by reliving each moment with you,
praying any witch can find a potion strong enough to brew
to exorcise this remorse that is now my reality.
You, gone, because a series of unfortunate events.
Now all I hear are the howls, echoes, and monsters
squealing. Entities conjured to keep me company
til' I see you again.

When it's time to depart this haunted house,
I carry emotions wary. We had heaven together,
so this must be hell. What a story we have to tell.

Two lovers separated from deaths kiss in the darkness.
Heartless.
I'll meet you somewhere between
chaos *and* **midnight.**

I'll meet you where the sun flares hit our ozone.
*There **our love** will be set ablaze.*
There is where we will draw each ounce of warmth from
one another.
It's there our love will burn in brilliance
to a new beginning.

Unfortunately the most unsightly of scars are worn by the
most beautiful of souls, and pain is carried by the most
undeserving of people.
But yet they carry it with vigor,
and wear these scars ***unpretentious.***

When this denial disappears
and your death becomes real,
I don't know how I'm going to survive,
feeling the pain.
I'll never get to touch you again —
*the absolute **love of my life**.*

My heart still bleeds for you
and yearns for your kiss.
Your embrace was the ultimate bliss.

The words pierce my skin as I say aloud
"I'll never see him again."
Those words to others are sad.

No one but me will live with the agony
of what never touching you again will entail.

Your death is a dark vision I will never accept,
But I cannot deny it.
It really happened.

Torment, *I'm now trapped in.*

I love you today as much as yesterday,
and I'll love you the same *tomorrow*.
I can't comprehend, when losing you starts
to feel real, how trapped I will be in utter *sorrow*.

Our love is a bond that can't be broken
no matter how far it bends.
You and I, no matter how far,
will **transcend.**

And one day we will sit at a banquet of confession,
having to spill our sins.
And my greatest wrong doing will be every
misdeed I committed in attempt to save you.
My vice I'd commit twice,
because loving you too much will be my
condemnation.
I will suffer for eternity for a love I cherish enduringly.

When I lost you I lost half of me,
but I was also half of you.
So when death stole you, you took a piece of me with you.
*Now I'm living in the **in between**.*

The day you left became the emptiness
between the *stars* and the earth.

The nothingness that lingers but a long journey.
Memories build a staircase, one heartache at a time.
Each step is created as I walk alone trying to reach you,
out of billions of *stars.*

I will always be able to find you, with love fueling me.
I'll search for your light; that aura of light I know
instinctively
and when the time is right, *I'll become a **nova**.*
I'll forever be pulled into your orbit,
as we shine in conjunction,
forever circling a love I will
eternally be pulled towards.

I know one thing.
As sure as the tide will continuously rise,
whether I am here or not,
*I was made **to love you.***
And while I'm here, that is exactly what I'll do.

Because in the end,
through the good and bad,
you were still by my side.
With that, I can know our love will still grow old…
even if we can't be together.

I have to extinguish this deep flame of anger I hold
within for all the people, especially one person who did me
the worst, *(the one who **enabled** you.)*
There was a passion to get revenge.
I was set ablaze by an intense vengeance.
If I don't extinguish it, I feel the hatred I carry for all
those who hurt me will burn this entire world to the
ground.

Or maybe if I set these feelings scorching straight to the
person who did me the worst, *I'll be set **free**.*
Her destiny is amongst the flames.

Either way, for the injustice she's done to those she could
have saved, instead let turn cold,
*then **burn**.*

Oh how I yearn to see the day she learns
her fate,
and that not all is forgiven.

There's something I need to tell you.
Though the ending was not what we had planned,
I need you to know I'm so very proud of how hard
you tried.
You beat yourself up, ***black and blue***,
fighting demons and battles that I can't even comprehend
(of addiction.)
All for the chance to be able to see each one of your
dreams come true.

You fought so hard,
and I will always be extremely proud of the man that you
became in such a short time.

*You made all of **my dreams come true**.*

You weren't perfect, but that's exactly what I loved
about you. You didn't try to be perfect, you tried to
he ***human***.
But being human in this world that we live in
is difficult.

The truth about everything is that you just loved and felt
everything too intensely; had such a passion inside of you
that you didn't know how to put those feelings into an
outlet.
You held them all in and it became too much for you to
bare, but still.. I'm so extremely proud of the human that
you became.

You grew into a man so quickly, and I will never forget the
strength that you showed, fighting for who you wanted to
be;
fighting to a life that felt **worthy.**

You almost had it all, but your demons called,
and one fatal mistake carried you away.
But you are not your mistake.
Through every rise and fall,
I hope you know, *it was an honor* **loving you.**

I had you in ways my mind can only articulate.
I had all of you, as infinitely as space expands,
then none of you, as time slipped through my hands.

Take me back to the night we first met.

You were meant to fly.
Fly free of life's tragedies;
free of life's unfair circumstances.
Like the melody of your life's song —
a song I wish I could've prolonged.

You float all around me,
like feathers dancing intricately to
your old life's tune;
ornately surrounding me with your
scent to remind you're still here.
So I'll close my eyes and kiss the air.

Devour me with the same intensity
of a solar flare.

I need to be absorbed by you,
even if it's by your ghost.

Like our favorite quote,
"be with me always"
in all ways indestructible;
in ways unseen.

The place we spent most of our time was your bed.
Where friendship turned into love
and love then turned into lessons,
Where we grew adjacent,
then apart,
then back together, even closer…
our souls consolidated.

We learned from each other.
Where two hearts inevitably collided,
we laughed and cried.
We didn't just make love,
*we made a **small eternity**.*
We faltered; we thrived.

All from this tiny room,
our love, it bloomed.

I had all of you, in our room;
in our cozy cocoon.

That was then; this is now.
Oh how life is profound.

You left, and I miss our life and the bed
you'd kiss me goodnight in.
We had a tiny room with a bed full of
big dreams.

A part of me will always be in that bed
with you, it seems.
Though you left in spirit with so much left unsaid,
I left part of me embedded,
due to a fate I dreaded.

You were cremated,
one ember at a time my dreams faded.
Fire stealing the love inside, turning me so cold.
I swear the smoke from that day found me
and clouded every thought.

A bad decision took you away,
 and all I can say is your death,
it started a chain of events
that slowly stripped me of the person I was.

*Once happy, **now shattered;***
*death stole all that truly **mattered.***

I mourn you
and I mourn the life we missed out on.
I mourn the days you will miss, and your kiss;
I mourn birthdays and holidays; the days that I'll search,
but never find your face.

You are inevitably the one person I can never replace.

There is a true void, like a black hole
that slowly engulfs you from within.
How can a love so strong; a person so beautiful
and full of life now be in a box?
That day for me, *time stopped.*
Mentally to me, we will forever be 32,
harboring a love so undeniably true.
I can't grasp the concept of this —
all the meaning or purpose behind it.

I have to submit to the darkness and pray
when I reach out my hand in the void and plead,
you'll reach back for me.
I'll welcome the shadows ,for that is now
where amongst the silent squalls,
your spirit calls.
I love you, always, for all days
signed,
—— *the girl you left behind.*

I taught my daughter that her daddy
lives in the sky.
She is not old enough yet to ask why.
I dread the day I will have to say
"drugs are bad,"
and took daddy away.
Explaining to her
that's where he has to stay.
That he won't be back for holidays.
That he won't see her grow up.
That he won't dance with her nights,
giggling and playing.
That she won't hear his laugh
or his favorite sayings.
I explained daddy, he's with you,
watching you,
everyday, *always.*
Never doubt his love for you,
because you were undoubtedly
his dream come true.
And now I will guide you.

You'll always have your daddy,
Just look up.
Talk to him.
He's there.

I cling to my grief like the branches of a weeping willow, heavy weight weighing me down, but now the only part of you I have left in me.

I'm deep rooted in sorrow, but clinging to anything that brings me back to the days I felt you as beautifully as the wind swaying through these branches.

I am now transforming into this weeping willow, seeping tears into the soil, watering this grief
because it's the only reminder
you existed.

175

And though we didn't get our happy ending,
it's our story that brings a tear to my eye.
It's the moments between the beginning and the end that
fill my heart with gratitude.
Not everyone gets to experience a love so true.

With a kiss sent to the heavens,
I will revel in the bliss we once shared and remember as
delicately as a bee carries pollen against the wind, we
fought against all odds to make a love worthy of miracles.

I will carry you and our story in my heart every moment,
every kiss, every second of it, and always wonder and
daydream
what a... *happy ending*.. might've been like.

I thought I was enough.
Enough to break the cycles of bad behavior.
I thought I could actually love the hurt out of you.
I thought our love was enough to conquer it all together,
but I soon found out I was wrong.

I thought I was enough,
but what I didn't realize is you weren't trying to feel more.
You searched for something
*to make you feel **less**.*

There will never be a perfect day to say goodbye.
There will never be a moment or second in time that
I feel I will be ready to let go.
I will always be holding on.
I'm not even exactly sure to what.
Maybe the thought that if reincarnation is real,
that we will both be reborn into a life
*where this time **we get it right.***

One day we will share a tomb,
and thats when we will take our love to the grave.
I will one day lay with you for all of *eternity.*
And I know with full certainty, thats the forever I
want.
*To be **anywhere** and **everywhere** with
you.*

Meet the author:

Jessica Livia, also known as MLIVV,
is an author, poet, single mother, and widow who believes
in expressing herself through the magic of poetic words.
She writes to share with the world her belief that there is a
such thing as love after death, for love never truly dies.

To get to know the author, follow her on her social media
accounts:

Instagram: @mlivvpoet
Tiktok: @mlivvpoet

Acknowledgements:

To my Matina:
My little girl, you are forever the best of me. You saved my life in every way possible. You are an absolute miracle and you will always be what I am most proud of. Mommy loves you beyond the stars and beyond the galaxies. I love you to infinity.

To my father:
My first love, thank you for the beautiful life that you have given to me and continue to. You are an amazing pop-pop. I love you so much.

To my brother:
You are undoubtedly the perfect guy in every aspect. You are my idol and I'm extremely grateful for you stepping in to help me raise my daughter. I know if she has you as far as this life goes, she has everything. And I cannot be more honored for her to grow up loving you.

To my mom:
You are undeniably the most beautiful woman I've ever met on the inside and out. You are my best friend, the person that has been there for me, by my side, every second. I don't know how to do life without you. Thank you for being the best Nana, the best mom, and the best woman I've ever met in my life. I strive to be like you. I love you mommy. Thank you for doing life with me.

To my aunt Lucy: You are seriously an angel on earth. You filled my childhood and my life with memories I can never thank you enough for. Thank you for always being my second mom. I love you more than words can express.

To my Nonna Livia: I miss you every day. You made me the better person that I am today. Thank you for leaving me your strength and guiding me this past year, since you have been gone. Continue to watch over me. I love you so much.

Octave
Eight
PUBLISHING
∞

octaveeightpublishing@gmail.com